What or Who is God?

Aurora knew that God was different from us humans but she couldn't quite understand how.

Lady Kimberly Motes Doty

ISBN 979-8-8690-2700-9 (paperback)
ISBN 979-8-8690-2701-6 (digital)

Lady Kimberly industries LLC
15019 Madeira Way, #86174
Madeira Beach, Florida 33708-9998

https://mybook.to/LadyKimberlyBooks

This Page is Intentionally Left Blank

Once upon a time, there was a curious and kind-hearted girl named Aurora.

She loved asking questions and exploring the world around her.

One day, as she sat under a big apple tree, she looked up at the sky and wondered, "What or who is God?"

Aurora knew that God was different from us humans, but she couldn't quite understand how.

So, she decided to embark on an exciting journey to discover who God really is.

As Aurora searched for answers, she met many wise and helpful people who shared their thoughts with her.

They told her that God is like a spirit.

But what does that mean?To help Aurora understand, they told her a story about a magical invisible friend.

This friend couldn't be seen, but you could feel their love and presence all around you.

Just like the wind that you can't see, but you can feel it gently blowing against your face.

Just like the way the wind blows the leaves and flower petals around when you are playing outside.

He is always with us.

We can talk to Him in our hearts and He listens to us.

Aurora's eyes widened with excitement as she realized that she could talk to God anytime she wanted.

God's purpose is to create a world filled with love, joy, and happiness, and to guide and care for us along the way.

He wants us to live our lives with kindness, respect, and compassion towards others.

She felt comforted knowing that God was always there, watching over her and listening to her thoughts and prayers.

With this newfound understanding, Aurora continued her journey, eagerly exploring more about God and His love for all of us.

And so, dear reader, just like Aurora, you too can discover who God is.

Remember, He is like a friendly invisible friend, always by your side.

You can talk to Him in your heart, and He will listen.

God is a Spirt: and they that worship him must worship him in spirit and in truth.

John 4:24 King James Version

About the Author

Lady Kimberly Motes Doty has dedicated her life to helping people in many different ways. She is a minister, which means she helps others find their spiritual path. She is also a life coach, which means she guides people to live their best lives. Lady Kimberly is even a natural health specialist, which means she knows a lot about taking care of our bodies and staying healthy. In addition to all of this, she loves to write and share her wisdom with others. When she's not working, she enjoys spending time with her family.

https://mybook.to/LadyKimberlyBooks

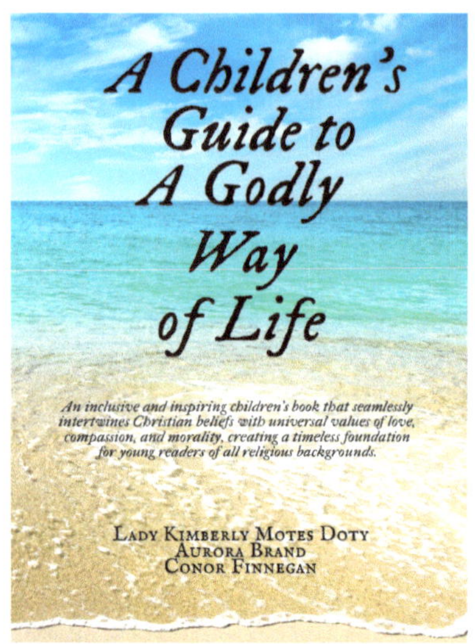

More Lady Kimberly Children's Books for you to enjoy!

Children's Guide to a Godly Way of Life is not just another ordinary book. It is a treasure trove of knowledge and wonder, carefully crafted to quench the thirst for understanding that resides within every child's soul. With each turn of the page, their imagination will ignite, propelling them on a lifelong voyage of love and devotion to God, and an insatiable hunger for unraveling the mysteries of the divine.

Introducing a captivating and educational new children's book series by the talented author, Lady Kimberly Motes Doty. This incredible series aims to teach children about God's love and His teachings from the Bible through meaningful and relatable short stories. Lady Kimberly Motes Doty has beautifully crafted each book to be Biblically based and easy for children to understand, ensuring that young readers can grasp the profound messages within.

The first book in the series, "What or Who is God?", tackles the age-old question that has puzzled minds throughout history. Lady Kimberly Motes Doty introduces children to the concept of God in a gentle and relatable way, encouraging them to ask questions and explore their curiosity. Through this book, children will develop a personal connection with God, enabling them to understand His presence in their lives.

Following this, "Where is God?" takes young readers on a journey of discovery, highlighting the beauty of God's presence in everyday life. Lady Kimberly Motes Doty reminds children that although God may not be seen with physical eyes, His love and guidance are always there, waiting to be discovered in the wonders of the world and the kindness of others. This heartwarming story inspires children to explore their own connection with God, fostering a sense of awe and gratitude.

In "Does God Lie?", Lady Kimberly Motes Doty invites readers to embrace the truth that God's promises are like a treasure chest filled with love, peace, and hope. This heartwarming story reassures children that in a world filled with uncertainties, they can find solace and strength in the unwavering faithfulness of God. Through relatable characters and engaging storytelling, young readers will learn the importance of trust and the power of God's word.

Continuing the series, "Is Everything God Does Good?" explores the beauty and love found in God's creations, emphasizing the importance of being good stewards of the natural world. Lady Kimberly Motes Doty's delightful tale encourages children to appreciate and respect the wonders of the world, fostering a sense of responsibility and gratitude for God's creations.

The Last book in the initial release is, "What Are Angels?" which captivates young readers with its exploration of angels and their role in our lives. Through the eyes of a curious little boy named Cade, Lady Kimberly Motes Doty takes children on a journey of discovery and understanding. Cade's fascination with angels leads him to ask his mother about their purpose and how they keep us safe. In response, his loving mother imparts wisdom and shares stories from the Bible, explaining that angels are invisible superheroes sent by God to watch over and protect us. This enchanting story instills a sense of wonder and reassurance in children, reminding them of the divine presence that surrounds them.

Lady Kimberly Motes Doty's children's book series, Discovering God's Love, is a true gift to young readers, offering them the opportunity to develop a deep understanding of God's love and teachings in a language they can comprehend.

Each book in the series presents important lessons in an accessible and engaging manner, nurturing children's spiritual growth and fostering a lifelong connection with God.

With these captivating and educational stories, Lady Kimberly Motes Doty has created a series that will undoubtedly become a cherished addition to every child's library.

The second release in Lady Kimberly's series, "Discovering God's Love" begins with "Is Anger Bad?". It is a charming tale that teaches children about the power of anger and how to handle it wisely. Through relatable characters and captivating storytelling, this book empowers young readers to embrace their emotions and make a positive impact on the world.

It continues with the uplifting children's book, "What is God's Greatest Commandment?" takes readers on another journey with the three curious and compassionate cousins Aurora, Conor, and Cade. One day, while playing near a majestic oak tree, they happen upon a special book called the Bible. As they open its pages, they discover the concept of commandments - rules given by God to guide them in living a purposeful and fulfilling life. Driven by their newfound understanding, Aurora, Conor, and Cade embark on a mission to put these commandments into action in their daily lives.

Lady Kimberly has many more books planned for the Discovering God's Love children's book series.

The Bible contains over 600 verses with commandments in the verses and some of the verses have multiple commandments in each verse!

Lady Kimberly and her grandchildren have an unlimited imagination to fill the pages for young readers!

When the series is completed, all of the books will be available in English, Spanish and French at least. The possibility of other languages is always open!

If the Alphabet Grew Out of The Sea V1 - in English, French & Spanish

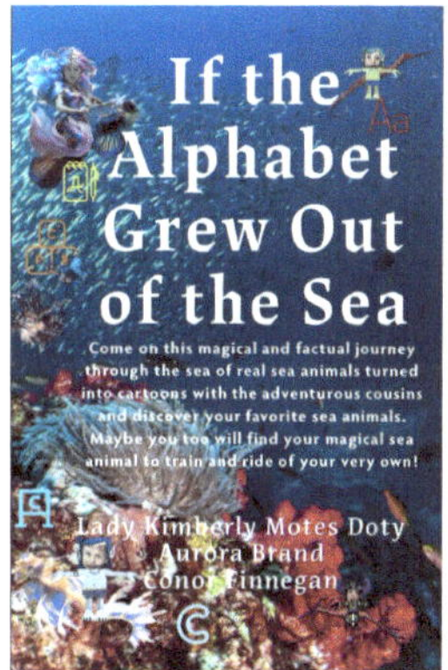

Version 2 has almost 600 pages of mazes, word searches and fun sea animal facts as Aurora, Conor and Cade search for sea animals for every letter of the Alphabet!

Embark on an enchanting adventure with Conor and his wise grandmother, Mimi. Join them on a treasure hunt for the fabled Conch shell, rumored to possess a magical sound. This heartwarming tale explores the power of love and the enchantment found in simple moments. Inspired by their journey, Conor and Mimi's story inspires others to embark on their own adventures and treasure hunts. Discover the magic within the pages of "Conor's Magical Treasure Hunt.

Coming soon:

"The Treasure Hunters: A Beachcombing Adventure"

Embark on an unforgettable beachcombing adventure with Aurora, Cade, and their beloved Mamaw. Join these adventurous siblings as they search for hidden treasures washed up by a powerful storm. From sand dollars to seashells, their journey is filled with wonder, joy, and the bonds of family. Discover the magic of exploration and the beauty of the ocean in "The Treasure Hunters: A Beachcombing Adventure."

"The Enchanted Seashell: A Magical Beach Adventure"

The Enchanted Seashell: A Magical Beach Adventure is a heartwarming children's book that takes young readers on an enchanting journey filled with wonder, discovery, and the power of love and resilience. Join Cade and Aurora as they embark on a treasure hunt to find the largest sand dollar ever. Along the way, they learn valuable lessons about patience, the beauty of nature, and the importance of ocean conservation. This captivating tale inspires children to appreciate the wonders of the world and make a positive impact on the planet.